# REVIEWS

"This is a groundbreaking and thought-provoking play, which must be seen. It frames the stories of people who lived through turbulent times, during the race riots of 1919 in Wales.

Ndidi John skilfully brings characters from the past into relevant three-dimensional focus. She outlines and breathes life into both Black and White protagonists and also uses gender and sexism as a lens, reflecting on a time when women as well as Black and Global majority people experienced struggle and inequity.

Although set in 1919, the play has stark parallels with society today. The central themes of mistrust, racism and yearning to belong - are still sadly apparent. We therefore need to look to the past, in order to learn. Ndidi's work gives us the opportunity to reflect, and food for thought, on the importance of acceptance, tolerance and kindness. All things which are so vital in our shared humanity."

**Dr Susan Davis**
**Reader in Diversity Equity and Inclusion in Education**
**Cardiff Metropolitan University.**

# ROUTES

1919 Race Riots – War Doesn't Always Beget Peace

A PLAY

BY

# NDIDI JOHN

STELLAR BOOKS

Published by:
Stellar Books
1 Birchdale
Bowdon
Cheshire
WA14 2PW, UK

www.stellarbooks.co.uk

ISBN: 978-1-910275-337

Published in 2023.

A catalogue record for this book is available at the British Library.

Designed and typeset in Open Sans and Seaford by Stellar Books

Cover artwork by Gerallt Hughes:  Instagram: scatterdrain_art

FSC is a non-profit international organisation established to promote responsible management of the world's forests. Products carrying the FSC label are independently certified to assure consumers that they come from forests that are managed to meet the social economic and ecological needs of present and future generation.

To my parents, who planted seeds of knowledge.
And nurtured them,
Who convinced me I could change the world,
And taught me the power of the pen.

To my siblings, the rocks upon which I stand,
My Guard*ian* angel through life's demands.
My Bother, Sido, an inspiration,
And proof that anyone can!

To Hope, my motivation,
And reason for writing this play,
May you always rise, like a phoenix from the ashes,
To fight another day.

For the brave unsung heroes,
Who's memories dwell in the shadows,
To my readers who breathe life into this history.
To tomorrow's unspoken stories.

To the younger me, who dared to dream,
And refused to go unseen.
May I soar on wings like eagles,
Run and never grow weary.

# DRAMATIS PERSONAE

**Rose**     Black Caribbean, female, 40+. A wise, courageous woman. Rose was made a widow during the war, and now singlehandedly runs a boarding house on the bustling streets of Butetown. She is a well-respected by the local community and is not afraid of anybody.

**Bethan**   White, female, Welsh, 25+. Courageous, but anxious, trapped on the wrong side of the race riots. Under constant attack, Bethan stands on hr morals and takes a stand to prove her loyalty and love for Raphael.

**Raphael**  Black Caribbean, male, 30+. Both a pillar of the community and an aggressor. Determined in his fight for justice, Raphael will stop at nothing, and does not fear anybody. A natural born leader, and a headman during the riots.

**Rufus**     Black Caribbean, male, 30+. Eccentric, subservient, and often impetuous. Rufus is Raphael's right-hand man. Many fear his spontaneous, erratic nature.

**Vaughan**   White, male, Welsh, 30+. Bethan's older brother. Arrogant, devious and valiant. His bold personality makes him a force not to be reckoned with.

**Gladys**    Black Caribbean, female, 0-3 months. Rose's granddaughter.

# SCENE ONE

A Butetown boarding house - June 12th, 1919.

*ENTER* **Rose and Bethan**

*A glimmer of light breaks into the living room through a broken window. Rose stands amidst the glass in the dead of the night. A violent struggle can be heard from upstairs. Rose does not flinch as the commotion travels down the stairs.*

*Bethan is thrown into the room and stumbles to the ground. She is badly beaten, her house coat stained with blood.*

*Rose throws a look of disgust to Bethan before raising her head, straining to hear the inaudible voices of angry men as the commotion continues upstairs. A stampede of footsteps descends the stairs and fade away from the house.*

*Rose pauses at the living room door, plucking up the courage to open it.*

*EXIT* **Rose**

*Bethan is alone in the living room, anxious, panicked. She skulks into the shadows of the room, breathing uncontrollably.*

*ENTER* **Rose** and **Raphael**

*Rose struggles to support Raphael over her shoulder. She collapses him onto the floor and checks him over for major wounds. Bethan watches from a distance, scared to advance.*

*Rose rushes to the chest of drawers, pulling a drawer to the floor in a hurried attempt to find scissors amongst the contents strewn on the floor. She takes a firm grip of the scissors and advances towards Bethan, grabbing her by the scruff of her house coat. Bethan fears for her life.*

*Rose makes a cut in the housecoat and tears a long strip from it. She demolishes the drawer on the floor with her foot and takes a large piece of wood from the remains.*

*Back by Raphael's side, Rose lifts his arm with caution and places it on the wood, wrapping the material around it to make a splint for his broken arm.*

*Relieved, Bethan advances to help, but a hard, cold stare from Rose stops her in her tracks. Raphael groans in pain. Rose lifts his head and encourages him to speak.*

**Raphael:**    Bet'an?

*Rose looks down on Raphael with disdain. She moves away to make room for Bethan, who collapses beside him, stroking his face, avoiding his bleeding wounds.*

*Rose stares out of the broken window then turns her attention to the living room which has been turned upside down; almost everything is broken.*

*Raphael struggles to steady himself on his elbow. He looks past Bethan noticing the state of the living room for the first time.*

**Raphael:**   Rose?

*Rose glares at Raphael for a moment then turns her back.*

BLACKOUT

# SCENE TWO

*ENTER* **Rose, Raphael** *and* **Bethan.**

*Raphael pulls himself into a chair. He spits onto a piece of cloth and uses it to clean a cut on his face in the reflection of a broken dirty piece of glass. Rose assembles unbroken trinkets as she sweeps broken glass into the corner. Bethan stands idle, awkward.*

**Rose:**      You should never have brought this white woman into my house.

**Raphael:**   I'm going to find the men dat did this. Dem dare come in here? I'll replace everything dem mash up.

**Rose:**      With what? You're weeks behind with your board already, and now it's furniture you buying? Dem driving our men off the docks every day. Why you act so foolish? You can't see what you've done, 'cause of this?

*Rose points at Bethan with disgust.*

**Bethan:**    I will contribute towards...

**Rose:** (Enraged) Woman, don't open your mouth in this house. You should have kept your little fancy self beyond the bridge where you belong; you have no business 'ere. There are rules. But you, with one greed 'pon you, can't help yourself, and look at what you've done. I wouldn't accept your stinking money, even if it was to bring my late husband back from the dead.

**Raphael:** Rose!

*Rose throws a deadly glare across the room silencing Raphael. He collapses back into the chair, wincing in pain. Bethan has not moved or cowered away from Rose; she stands her ground in silence.*

**Bethan:** It's ok, Rapha.

**Rose:** It's not ok!

*Rose moves to the window.*

**Rose:** For all you know dem men who beat you so are out there watching over this house.

**Raphael:** Come from there, Rose.

**Rose:** Waiting to come back in 'ere. Wondering why the hell she hasn't left this place.

**Raphael:** (Shouts) Come from the window nah man!

*Rose ignores him.*

**Rose:**    What are you still doing 'ere as a matter of fact?

**Raphael:**    She's hurt. She can't go out there like dat.

**Rose:**    Raphael, hush your mouth. Look how dem mash you up. I thought you were smart and you come bring this foolishness to my house? I've a mind to throw both of you out on the street, let dem finish what dem started. I already warned you, don't bring no white woman into this house. So, don't tell me what I can or cannot do. Rules don't change for nobody, especially not her. Now get out of my house.

**Bethan:**    I'll leave. I'm not afraid to walk out there, I'll be fine.

**Raphael:**    You going to put her out on the street like that?

*Rose ignores Raphael and holds the door open for Bethan to leave. Raphael attempts to stand from the chair, staring at Rose. She doesn't look in his direction.*

**Raphael:**    I will walk you to the bridge.

**Rose:**    Don't move from dat chair. What's the matter with you? This woman turn you

stupid? Is your life you g'risk now? You
don't know who is waiting out there.

*A disturbance in the corridor startles them all. Rose and
Bethan back away from the door, panicked. Raphael
struggles to stand, letting out a loud groan. The door
bursts open.*

*ENTER* **Rufus** *fear set upon his face, brandishing a large
knife. He is relieved to see that everyone is ok, but
becomes enraged when he sees the state of the living
room and the extent of Raphael and Bethan's injuries.*

**Rufus:**    I see the front door broke up so, and the
window dem take out. You can see
straight in here from the street. Lord, me
nah want fi know what dem done in 'ere.
Wha' happen?

**Raphael:**    Is four of dem come. Dem hold me down
while them mash up Bet'an, drag her out,
and all four took dem time beating me so.

**Rose:**    (Frustrated) Is because of she! You lucky
dem nah follow you back in here. I don't
know why dem nah drag her dat bit
further onto the street. I'm a target in my
own house.

**Raphael:**    Rufus, walk Bet'an to the bridge. She has
to come out of here and...

**Rufus:**   Nothin' a go so, Rapha. This is just one of many boarding houses dem mash up, y'know? Is one whole heap of rioting go on out there.

**Raphael:**   What?

**Rufus:**   Over one hundred of dem, Rapha, over by the bridge fighting and so, police 'pon horse. Dem say one black man slit a white man's throat on Caroline Street, him dead already.

**Raphael:**   What you talking? Is a black man started all of this?

**Rufus:**   No, Sah. Dem say a white man attack one carriage 'pon road with black men and white women come back from some picnic. Dem mash dem up good, all of dem. Mohammed, send me, him call for you, him say come now. You and he must work out how you g'lead our men. We already gathering all the guns and knives we can find. Dem after we blood!

**Rose:**   Lord have mercy.

**Raphael:**   Help me up.

*Rufus supports Raphael under his arm.*

**Rose:** You can't go out there, Raphael. You can barely walk.

*Both men ignore Rose. Raphael struggles to find balance as they move towards the door.*

**Bethan**: Wait.

*Bethan removes her night coat and tears it down the middle. She wraps it around Raphael's rib cage, tucking it into his shirt trapping the splint on his arm.*

**Rufus**: We can reach Mohammad's, it's nowhere near the bridge. I'll help him, Miss Rose.

**Raphael:** Rufus, go upstairs and get my gun from the drawer.

*EXIT* **Rufus**

**Raphael:** Listen hard. Both of y'all stay put, do y'hear? You don't leave this house! And Rose, she better be here when I get back.

*Bethan unties the splint and re-wraps it. Rose kisses her teeth and turns away.*

*ENTER* **Rufus**

**Rufus:** (Flustered) It's not there! Dem must have take it.

**Rose:** Take Gregory gun. It's in the kitchen deh.

**Raphael:** No, you need dat 'ere. Is a knife all you have 'pon you, Rufus?

**Rose:** The good Lord will protect me. Me nah g'pull a gun 'pon nobody.

**Raphael:** (Stern) It stays here! Come, Rufus.

*Rufus helps Raphael out of the door.*

**Rose:** Did you see my Neci out there? Find her and bring her back. You hear me, Rufus?

**Rufus:** Yes, Miss Rose. Someone will have her; is everyone look to Neci.

**Rose**: Just find her.

**Raphael:** Barricade the door and stay away from the window. Rose?

*Rose gestures to acknowledge the instruction. Raphael attempts to touch Bethan's face, but she pushes his hand away.*


*EXIT* **Raphael** *and* **Rufus**

# SCENE THREE

*There's an awkward silence as Rose scans the room. She grabs the base of the sofa, struggling to drag it across the floor.*

**Bethan:** Let me help you.

*Rose throws Bethan a disapproving glance.*

**Bethan:** It's heavy. Rose?

**Rose:** Don't call my name. You don't know me....... You don't know me.

**Bethan:** Fine. But this will be done much quicker with the two of us.

**Rose:** You think this is the first time I have to lug stuff around here? Everything I do is on my own. Move!

*Bethan, ignores Rose, grabbing the other end of the sofa.*

*Rose cuts her eye at Bethan and lets go, leaving her to position the sofa in front of the door alone. It's a heavy struggle but Bethan manages it.*

**Bethan:**     I am sorry for the damage that has been done to your home, I truly am.

*Rose grabs another piece of furniture. Bethan struggles to make eye contact with her.*

**Bethan:**     But I will not apologise for my relationship with Rapha.

*Rose hums an old tune to drown out the sound of Bethan's voice.*

**Bethan:**     We love each other, and you can't help who you love. (Pause) I know how you must feel about me. I...

**Rose:**     (Enraged) Don't dare tell me how I feel. You don't know a damn thing about me or anyone else around here. You come and see our men and women dancing and cackling in dem drinking dens, and it take your fancy. But you know what you don't see? The killer river running through all of dem of blood, sweat and tears from the hard work dem give here, and for what?

You nah hear him tell you is a riot out there? And here you are filling my head with talk o' love? The war isn't over for us y'know, it's just beginning, so stop your fairytale nonsense, idiot woman. You better pray to God dat your 'love' make it out of this alive, and nah end up dead and buried with the rest of dem.

**Bethan:**     Rapha is smart...

**Rose:**     My husband was smart, but no man can think faster than a bullet. (Pause...)
Is your people do this.

*Rose points to the destruction in the room.*

**Rose:**     Is your people by the bridge fighting to come through here. Dem hate us. So, excuse me if I'm finding it difficult to like you.

**Bethan:**     They're not my people, I'm not like them.

**Rose:**     You are just like dem. Why is this place mash up so, eh? Because you think you're better and you have no respect, because when I said 'no' you tell yourself 'yes', and here you are... And now here I am.

**Bethan:**     I don't think like them, and I don't think I'm superior to you, or anyone. We had nowhere else to go.

**Rose:**     Woman! What does that tell you? You're not supposed to be. Dem trying to force us out of this country, repatriate us, paying us to leave. Dem nah want to see us settling down especially with no white people. If you really love Raphael let him go. It's hard enough round here.

**Bethan:** I'm surprised you think that way. You don't strike me as the sort of woman to back out of a fight for equality, but I surely won't allow anyone to determine my future based on their racist, backward thinking.

**Rose:** Is me you call a racist?

**Bethan:** No, I was referring to them, but forgive me for saying, you're no better.

*Rose advances on Bethan. Pointing directly into her face.*

**Rose:** Woman, I won't hesitate to mash you up in here, you nah? Your mouth too fast.

*Bethan doesn't retaliate. She stands stern but calm.*

**Rose:** You make me sick, you and your righteous self. I should...

*Both women are startled as the living room door is forced open.*

# SCENE FOUR

---

*ENTER* **Raphael** *pushing his weight against the barricaded door.*

**Raphael:**   (In haste)  Rose, help me with this, come.

*Rose backs away from Bethan. They pull the chair from the door.*

**Raphael:**   What's going on?

*Both women stand in silence.*

**Raphael:**   Rose? Bethan?

**Bethan:**   Nothing. Is it bad out there?

**Rose:**   Where's Rufus?

*Raphael unzips his coat and prepares his arms to support* **Gladys** *wrapped in a cotton blanket.*

**Raphael:**   He's taking some of the women to the church, dem gathering there now. Is enough places dem mash up round here! Rose, Neci is sick. She got licked with the flu last night. Dem took the baby from her but...

**Rose:**      Lord my God. Where is she?

**Raphael:**    Miss Kitty have her at the......

*Rose rushes to take Gladys from Raphael but he pulls her out of her reach.*

**Raphael:**    No, Rose, let Bet'an take Gladys. Is something wrong?

**Rose:**      Over my dead body is she laying a hand p'on that child, what's the matter with you?

*Rose stretches out her arms to take Gladys.*

**Rose:**      Go get Neci.

**Bethan:**    I'm a nurse, let me look at her.

**Rose:**      Raphael, pass me my grandchild, y'hear? You have children?

**Bethan:**    No.

**Rose:**      Is two children I raised. Move!

*Rose takes the baby from Raphael.*

**Raphael:**    Rose, let her take......

**Rose:**      This woman will not come near dis child. Me nah trust her; is your woman dat.

*Rose turns away and examines Gladys' face.*

**Rose:**       Lord, look at this child. What dem said?

**Raphael:**   She won't eat, drink or even cry. She's just weak so.

**Rose:**       ...and Neci?

**Bethan:**    When was her last feed?

**Raphael:**   Yesterday morning.

**Rose:**       What about Neci?

**Bethan:**    Is she drinking? Does she have a temperature?

**Rose:**       She's going to be fine.

**Raphael:**   Rose, the child sick!

**Rose:**       (Perturbed) She's going to be fine.

**Raphael:**    I must go back.

**Rose:**       No! You get my Neci, bring her back here.

**Bethan:**    It's better to keep her away from the baby. This pandemic is not...

**Rose:**       Mind your business. There's room enough in this house for dat. I want my daughter home.

**Raphael:**   She's too sick, Rose.

**Rose:**    (Desperate) What you expect me to do, eh? You know how many people me see this wicked flu leave fi dead? Bring back my Neci! Is me she need now.

**Raphael:**    Come quick! I'll take you. Leave the baby with Bethan.

**Rose:**    I'm not leaving this wretched woman in my house! Bring Neci back here or don't come back.

*Rose turns her back on Raphael and Bethan, fighting back tears.*

**Bethan:**    Go! We'll be fine.

**Raphael:**    Did anyone come by here?

**Bethan:**    Nobody.

**Raphael:**    Close up this door. Do what you can.

*Raphael gestures towards Rose.*

**Bethan:**    I will. Go!

*Raphael and Bethan share a glance before he leaves.*

*EXIT* **Raphael.**

# SCENE FIVE

*Bethan pulls the furniture back into place. She stands idle for a moment.*

**Bethan:**   Can we not put our differences aside for the baby's sake? I can help you.

*Rose ignores Bethan. She hums a hymn to Gladys.*

*Bethan takes a drawer from the chest and folds the tablecloth, fitting it neatly inside. She places it on the chair.*

**Bethan:**   If she has a temperature your body heat may affect her. She'll be cooler in here.

*Rose finishes the song and sits on the broken chair with Gladys clutched close to her chest. Bethan sits on a chair across the room, looking towards the window.*

*The sound of the riots approaching cuts through the silence. Both women are anxious.*

**Rose:**   (to Gladys) If we were in the Caribbean, is no sickness like this y' know? We had everything on the yard there. Eucalyptus, the lime tree at the back, thistle, ....everything you need. One day I'll take you home and you will see for yourself. You, me, and my Neci. This place is a killer!

*Rose pulls Gladys away from her body in a panic.*

**Rose:**    Gladys... Gladys. She's shaking, what's the matter with her?

*Bethan rushes over and takes Gladys out of Rose's arms. She places her in the drawer and strips off a layer of clothing.*

**Bethan:**    It's a febrile seizure, we need to bring her temperature down. I need water.

**Rose:**    Ice? I can get ice?

**Bethan:**    No. We must bring the fever down gradually. Ice will make blood rush to her internal organs increasing her temperature. Get water, and a towel.

*Rose hesitates in fear.*

**Bethan:**    Go, Rose!

*Rose unblocks the door enough to slip out. Bethan shakes a photograph of a Rose's late husband, Gregory, in uniform from a broken frame on the floor and uses it to fan Gladys.*

**Bethan:**    Come on Gladys... Come on...

*Rose returns panicked carrying the water and a towel. She places it beside Bethan, dips the towel in the water and wrings it out.*

**Bethan:**   That's enough, leave some water in it.

*Rose hands the towel to Bethan.*

**Bethan:**   Here, fan her gently.

*Rose takes the photo and begins to fan Gladys. The two women are stood together tending to the baby.*

**Rose:**   Our Father, who art in heaven, hallowed be thy name. Thy Kingdom come, thiy will be done on earth as it is in Heaven...

*Bethan joins in the prayer in Welsh.*

**Rose:** Give us this day our daily bread, and forgive us our trespasses, as we forgive those who trespass against us. And lead us not into temptation, but deliver us from evil. For thine is the Kingdom, the power and the glory forever and ever. Amen.

**Bethan:** Dyro i ni heddiw ein bara beunyddiol, a maddau i ni ein dyledion fel y maddeuwn ninnau i'n dyledwyr, ac nac arwain ni ibrofedigaeth, eithr gwared ni rhag drwg, Canys eiddot ti yw'r deyrnas a'r nerth a'r gogoniant yn oes oesoedd. Amen.

*Rose stares at Gladys in the drawer. Bethan continues to moisten her face and body with water. She places her hand on Rose's arm to stop her fanning Gladys, and to calm her nerves.*

**Bethan:**     It's broken. She's going to be ok.

*Bethan moves away from Rose, and heads back to the chair, out of the way. Rose steps in front of the drawer and reaches in.*

**Bethan:**     Don't cover her. Her temperature is still dropping.

*Rose takes her hand out of the drawer.*

**Rose:**     Thank you.

**Bethan:**     She's not eating because she has a fever, though you must force her to drink. (Pause) You're welcome.

*Rose gestures toward the bowl of water and towel.*

**Rose:**     Clean yourself up.

**Bethan:**     I'm ok. Save it for Gladys, she may need it again.

*An awkward silence descends on the room.*

**Rose:**     Is in the Royal Hamadryad Hospital you work there?

**Bethan:** These past four years.

**Rose:** You know if them find out, your job gone?

*Bethan turns her back to Rose and walks towards the window.*

**Bethan:** I know.

**Rose:** You crazy.

**Bethan:** I'm determined.

**Rose:** It'll take a lot more than determination. Look at dem out there.

**Bethan:** Are you not worried about the men?

**Rose:** Worry does nothing but make you sick, child. Come away from the window!

**Bethan:** But Rapha...?

**Rose:** Raphael can take care of himself. Him and Mohammad will organised dem men and put a stop to this nonsense. When you catch dem two together...

**Bethan:** ...and if they don't?

**Rose:** Then you must thicken up like the rest of us. How many men you see come in the hospital there, and how many you see come out? Everybody leave somebody behind.

*Bethan grows anxious.*

**Rose:** You want me to tell you everything going to be fine? I can't do it. My husband gone, my daughter sick and look at my grandchild. Life is precious, but nobody is promised tomorrow. I'm sorry I can't offer you more dan dat.

**Bethan:** I'm sorry.

**Rose:** What for? I don't need your pity. Is we left here suffering. Better to be with the Creator than here in this hell, you understand?

*Bethan nods discerningly.*

**Rose:** Running around these streets with Raphael, trust me, it g'lead to nothing but trouble for you both. Make the most of the time you have 'pon this earth.

**Bethan:** This is me making the most of the time I have. (Pause) How is she?

*Rose reaches into the drawer and touches Gladys.*

**Rose:** Come.

*Bethan joins Rose beside Gladys and checks her temperature.*

**Bethan:**   Much better.

**Rose:**   I'll get her a drink.

**Bethan:**   No, leave her, she's settled. (Pause) Oh, to be a child!

**Rose:**   And live through all this again? No sah!

**Bethan:**   Who knows what the future holds for her.

**Rose:**   The future holds nothing but sickness and this; constant fighting and war. They should have left us in the Caribbean. She'd have had a good future there, let me tell you. Sometimes I must re-live dem days in my head to get me through.

**Bethan:**   Forgive me but if you hate it so much why not take the repatriation?

**Rose:**   This is my home now, is not any or anybody taking me out of here. Where me a go?

**Bethan:**   But...

**Rose:**   You know how hard I work to get where I am now? Boarding mistress of this house?

**Bethan:** But you make the Caribbean sound like paradise.

**Rose:** Um-hum! This is my paradise now. This is it!

**Bethan:** But surely...

**Rose:** Child, you is definitely trapped in some fairytale. You'll soon learn.

**Bethan:** I believe in fighting for what I want.

**Rose:** ...And when you have no fight left? I came here on a boat, convinced I was heading into a whole new world. Dem tell me opportunity... wealth... prosperity... all of dem things dem tell us. When I step off that boat in Liverpool... Boy! I don't know what hit me first... The frost biting off my face, or the bitter cold glare from all of dem there. I wanted to turn on my heels. I just knew. Don't ever go to that place, y' hear? It's wicked. Is one woman tell us about Cardiff. She say the coal go out, so the ship go out, and take plenty people. Well, we were gone.

I remember the first time I step foot in Butetown. I felt like I'd arrived home. The people here, the work, the spirit of this place. It wasn't half bad, so we decided to stay. Then Gregory went off to war and dat was dat.

We settle here now and dem no like it. Is nothing in the Caribbean for me. My family and friends are right here, if only they'd leave us be.

**Bethan:** I've never left Cardiff; I've had no reason to.

**Rose:** Child, you left Cardiff the moment you step foot inna Butetown. Dem are Caribbean streets out there. We made this place.

**Bethan:** It is quite different.

**Rose:** You don't know these streets. It's party, party you see here. You don't see, Miss Innis, she is one woman on her own, cooking twenty fish inna the morning to feed the men as dem pass. And she nah stand on the street with it, y'know? She leave her door open and dem eat till dem belly full. Miss Henry is the same. You don't see the real parties, fifty people in one house, the food, the punch, the dancing. You don't see all of dat. You have the same thing where you are over there?

**Bethan:** We don't have too many parties. There are plenty of dances to attend about town.

**Rose:** So, how you find yourself here, eh?

**Bethan:** Raphael brought me here the first time; I was quite scared. I've always been forbidden to come under the bridge.

**Rose:** Why, what's wrong with under the bridge?

**Bethan:** You said yourself, I have no business here. It's deemed unsafe for white women.

**Rose:** White women trail these streets all night long and make it out of here alive. Is the white men who are scared, not the women.

**Bethan:** People fear what they don't know.

**Rose:** The only thing them fear is not finding a decent job because we here, working hard, and doing well. That's what all of this is about. Dem mad to see us make a way for ourselves. Especially when dem see black men with white women, which is why you beat up so!

**Bethan:** Well, you can't blame them.

**Rose:** What?

**Bethan:** For being mad. They were promised the earth for their service in the war, and they've come home to a worse situation to when they left. They're angry.

**Rose:** I'm angry, but you don't see me running around the streets with a knife trying fi cut somebody. We didn't make dem those promises, so why they turn on us?

**Bethan:** Because, if you weren't here there would be enough jobs and accommodation for everyone.

*Rose, stares hard at Bethan.*

**Rose:** (Stern) Is that so?

**Bethan:** I didn't mean it like that.

**Rose:** Is exactly what you mean.

**Bethan:** Rose? Rose?

**Rose:** You see how you come in here? A wolf in sheep clothing.

**Bethan:** That's not true. There are two sides to every battle. I didn't say I agreed with it, I'm just stating a fact. You say I live in a fairytale, but you're no different:, hiding from the truth.

**Rose:** You better stop before I start my own riot up in 'ere.

**Bethan:** Then you'll be no better than them.

*Rose crosses the room coming face to face with Bethan.*

**Rose:** How dare you?

**Bethan:** Why are you so shocked? You've abused me since I was thrown in here, and for what? You've done nothing to them out there and they're attacking you. I've done nothing to you in here, and all you're doing is attacking me. Hence, I dare say you are just like them. They did this to me because I refused to leave, I stood up to those four men, so don't think I won't stand up to you. Beat me if it makes you feel better, it won't change a thing.

*Rose and Bethan hold a long, electric glare.*

**Rose:** Don't open your mouth in this house again.

**Bethan:** Why do you hate me so much?

**Rose:** I hate all of y'all. This is my house, I didn't invite you in here, and I don't want you here.

**Bethan:**   And that's exactly what they're saying about this country.

**Rose:**   But the only reason we're here is because you're there. You made yourselves real comfortable in the Caribbean and hoaxed us into this hell. So, what foolishness you talking? Is enough of our men died fighting for this country dat should be living well in the Caribbean, not dead and buried.

**Bethan:**   Rose, if I could...

*Their altercation is cut short by a commotion at the door. The women are startled.*

# SCENE SIX

*Bethan backs away from the door. Rose begins to pull away the barricade.*

**Rose:**       Raphael, is that you? You have my Neci?

*ENTER **Vaughan.** He forces the door open.*

*He grabs Rose by the neck, pressing a knife along her throat as he forces her backwards into the room. Bethan screams.*

**Bethan:**    Stopiwch! Gad hi fynd! (Stop it. Let her go!)

**Vaughan:**   Hi gwnaeth hwn i ti? (Did she do this to you?)

*He forces the knife deeper into Rose's neck.*

**Vaughan:**   Did she do this to you?

**Bethan:**    No! Na wnaeth hi ddim! (No, she didn't!)

**Vaughan:**   Don't be scared, you can tell me.

*Rose stands tall in Vaughan's grip, staring across the room.*

**Bethan:**    Vaughan!

*Rose and Vaughan lock eyes with Bethan.*

**Bethan:**    She didn't do it. A group of white men broke in here, they beat me to the ground, dragged me down the stairs.

*Vaughan releases Rose. He uses the blade of his knife to guide her into the broken chair, his eyes still fixed on Bethan, confused.*

**Vaughan:**  The men that came here did this?

**Bethan:**    Yes.

*Vaughan kicks over a piece of furniture in anger.*

**Vaughan:**  They should never have touched you.

*Bethan searches Vaughan's face, horrified.*

**Bethan:**    Did you send them?

**Vaughan:**  You have no business here with these aliens, Bethan.

**Bethan:**    Tell me you didn't do this.

**Vaughan:**  Where is he?

*Vaughan stands on guard, lifting his knife ready to defend himself.*

**Bethan:**    Why, Vaughan?

**Vaughan:**  Is he here?

**Bethan:**   What have you done?

**Vaughan:**   I sent them to come for you, and to teach him a lesson. Now you're here and he's gone. Did they take him? Bethan, you must tell me.

*Vaughan, grows anxious, pacing with his knife.*

**Bethan:**   How could you?

*Vaughan turns his knife on Rose.*

**Vaughan:**   Where is he? Tell me or I'll cut your throat.

*Rose sits still avoiding eye contact. Bethan, grabs his arm, pulling the knife away from Rose.*

**Bethan:**   You're behaving like an animal.

**Vaughan:**   Come on. We must get you back. They're closing in on this place, it's not safe.

*He beckons Rose to the window at knife edge.*

**Vaughan:**   You! Over there by the window where I can see you. Stay there and don't move.

*Vaughan heads for the door, holding out his hand.*

**Vaughan:**   Bethan?

**Bethan:**   I'm not leaving. 'm staying here.

**Vaughan:**   Like hell you are.

*Vaughan grabs Bethan again, pulling with force. She tries to resist him but his grip is too strong. She loses her footing and stumbles to the floor, forcing Vaughan to let go.*

**Bethan:**   No!

*Bethan stands to her feet and slides her hands across her stomach. She snaps her hands away when she notices Rose staring at her.*

**Vaughan:**  What are you doing? Men are rioting in the streets. You must get home.

**Bethan:**   I'm staying here.

*Rose looks down at Bethan's stomach. Bethan, panicked, stares back at Rose.*

**Vaughan:**  Bethan, there's no time. I know a way out.

*A disturbance in the corridor spurs Vaughan to cross the room. He tries to take Rose hostage, but she picks up a large piece of glass from the floor and thrusts it at him.*

*ENTER **Raphael** and **Rufus**, knives already poised. All five stand in silence assessing the consequences of their next actions. Raphael's eyes are locked on Vaughan, who looks from Rufus to Raphael, desperate to sense their next move.*

**Raphael:**   You ok, Rose?

**Rose:**       Um-hum!

**Raphael:**   Bet'an, this man hurt you?

*Bethan shakes her head.*

**Raphael:**   Rose, come here.

*Rose crosses the room keeping the broken glass between her and Vaughan. She stands between Raphael and Rufus, leaving Vaughan and Bethan on the other side of the room.*

*Raphael knocks the glass from Rose's hand and ushers her towards the baby.*

**Raphael:**   What's going on here?

**Bethan:**    He is my brother.

**Raphael:**   I don't care who he is when him have a knife pointing at my face. What is he doing in this house?

**Rose:**       Is him sent the men come f'beat you.

*Raphael, slowly advances on Vaughan, closely followed by Rufus.*

**Raphael:**   Is that so?

*Raphael rounds Vaughan, and kicks the back of his leg, sending him to his knees. Vaughan's knife falls out of his hand and Rufus picks it up. Raphael takes the knife from Rufus with his broken arm.*

**Raphael:** Rufus! Go get Mohammad. Tell him come.

**Rufus**: And leave you with him?

**Raphael:** Go!

*EXIT* **Rufus.**

**Raphael:** Is you sent dem men here?

*Vaughan is silent.*

**Bethan:** Rapha! Please don't hurt him.

**Raphael:** (Enraged) Look at me, Bet'an. You really expect me to let this man walk out of here?

**Bethan:** (Distressed) He's my brother.

**Raphael:** And look what him done to you.

**Vaughan:** They never should have touched her.

*Raphael, kicks Vaughan to the floor. Despite his vicious blows, Vaughan, remains straight-faced pulling himself back onto his knees.*

**Raphael:** Um-hum! Is me they come for? You have some nerve. You couldn't come yourself? You must end four men to fight me one? (Pause) What you come for?

**Vaughan:** I've come for my sister.

**Raphael:** Bet'an, you leaving with this man?

*Bethan's eyes fall to the floor.*

**Raphael:** She ain't going no place.

**Vaughan:** She's leaving with me.

**Raphael:** And where exactly do you think you're going?

**Vaughan:** They're closing in on this place.

*Raphael laughs.*

**Raphael:** You see all dem police out there? You really think it's us dem protecting why dem not letting y'all through? Is you dem protecting, 'cause once you step foot on these sides dem know we g'kill every single one of you. What's the matter with you people, eh?

**Bethan:** Rapha, I'm pleading with you.

**Raphael:** Shut up Bet'an, with your pleading. Look at this place. You crazy?

**Rose:** Her true colours shine now, eh?

**Bethan:** What do you expect me to do? Condemn my own brother to death?

**Raphael:** This man almost killed me in my own home.

**Bethan:** Not everything has to end in violence.

**Raphael:** So if it nah end in violence, how you expect it to end, heh?

*Bethan, stares back at Raphael.*

**Raphael:** Is dem out there causing trouble. What you expect us to do? Take a beating? I done dat already. Him mash me up, mash you up, mash up this place, and it's me you attack about violence? Let me deal with this. You people must think we're dogs, come f'kick us, thinking you're the masters of this place. What's your name?

**Bethan:** Vaughan.

**Raphael:** I want him to tell me!

*Vaughan continues to stare across the room, silent, enraged.*

**Raphael:** Your face looks familiar, where I know you from? You work down the docks? You over there on Milicent Street?

*Raphael nudges his knife closer to Vaughan's collar.*

**Bethan:** Vaughan, answer him.

**Raphael:**   Bet'an move over there.

**Bethan:**   No!

*Raphael fires a look at Bethan, but she stands her ground.*

**Rose:**   Is one fireball you find yourself there, Raphael.

*Raphael twists the blade of his knife into Vaughan's neck as he moves Bethan on with his eyes.*

*He uses the blade to lift Vaughan's head to get a better look at his face.*

**Raphael:**   Wait a minute. Is round here I've seen you, causing trouble as a matter of fact. Is that you?

*Vaughan doesnt flinch.*

**Raphael:**   I make you sick, ain't it? You know one thing I never understand? How we are the ones dat got betrayed and yet you all are trying to fight us.

**Vaughan:**   Betrayed?

**Raphael:**   Betrayed! Welcome us with open arms, one whole heap of blood sacrifice, then take up arms to force us out. You men are weak. This country! You couldn't fight dat war alone, so it's we you come for, and we came running! Of course we did! But before ink can dry 'pon Treaty, you want it all back, you want us out. Where you think we a go? Why you think some of our men are out there fighting in dem military uniform, eh? In case y'all ever forget, we have every right to be here. We fought together on dem ships, we're all in the same boat. There ain't no work for nobody, but we're all entitled to what little work there is left. We are a part of this empire now.

**Vaughan:** You will never be British. We built this country, our forefathers lay down those streets; centuries of work. You dare to claim that as your own?

**Raphael:** You stand so proud of your precious country but this metropole would be nothing without our colonies, you can't see dat? Is a pity flat roads and concrete is all y'all have to boast, 'cause where I come from is honour dat make a country, integrity, righteousness; not this foolishness!

What next, eh? Repatriation? (Laughs)

You think you smart. We have all of this, you want to send us home with nothing. Let me tell you, for every one of us you force out, is three of y'all dem g'murder when dem get back home, and you won't have police 'pon horse to protect you. 'Cause if we can't stay here after all we have done, is no way you staying there, sunning up yourselves and mek you feel real at home.

**Vaughan:** Why is it you people pull knives and guns at the first sign of a brawl, eh? Put your knife down and fight me like a man?

**Raphael:** Brawl is a you people thing. For us, this is nothing but self-defence. We nah trouble you, you came to Butetown looking this! Eh-eh! And if you wanted to fight me like a man, you one should have turned up here instead of those men you send to beat me so.

*Vaughan cautiously pushes one of Raphael's knives to one side with his hand.*

**Vaughan:** And if I'd have sent weapons such as this, you'd be a dead man.

*Raphael presses the knife into Vaughan's chest.*

# SCENE SEVEN

*ENTER **Rufus**. He stands panting for breath in the doorway, withdrawn.*

**Raphael:**   What?

*Panic sets upon Rose's face.*

**Rose:**        What happen, Rufus?

**Rufus:**       Mohammad. Them kill him out on the street.

**Raphael:**   What you talking about?

**Rufus:**       One wicked blow to the head.

*Rose collapses in the chair.*

**Rose**:        Lord have mercy!

**Rufus:**       Them rushed the police to get through. Was so fast Rapha, everyone fighting and the police lashing out, and him just go down.

**Raphael:**   You sure, Rufus? You know how dem fire news roun' here.

**Rufus:**   I saw it for myself; one crowd around him.

*Raphael is charged with anger. He kicks Vaughan to the floor and pushes the edge of his blade into his throat.*

**Raphael:**   Nobody ever do you nothing.

*Bethan starts towards the men. Rose tries to hold her back but she breaks free.*

**Bethan:**   Rapha, no!

*Raphael throws Bethan a piercing look.*

**Raphael:**   An eye for an eye, Bet'an.

**Bethan:**   Please!

*Bethan is distraught. Raphael, torn, kicks Vaughan in his gut, swiping the air with his knife in frustration. In the distraction, Bethan, attempts to help Vaughan, but Rufus, steps in to continue holding him at knife point.*

**Rufus:**   Let me deal with him, I'll sort him good. Mohammad gone. A whole heap of men out there look to you now. Go!

**Raphael:**   I ain't going no place till I deal with this.

*Raphael moves Rufus out of the way and resumes his position in front of Vaughan.*

**Rufus:**   Dem wild with rage out there since Mohammad...

**Raphael:**    Good!

**Rufus:**    No Rapha, them nah know what dem do! You can't waste no time. Dem need you out there.

*Raphael continues to stare at Vaughan.*

**Rufus:**    Rapha? You nah hear me talk to you? Do it! Ain't nobody got time for this.

**Raphael:**    Shut up, Rufus.

**Rufus:**    What's the matter with you? What you hesitating for?

**Bethan:**    Rufus?

**Rufus:**    Woman, is man's business this?

**Rafael:**    (Shouts) Rufus

**Rufus:**    Stop calling me and deal with the thing nah man, before you make me rage up in here. They're killing our men out there: you should have slit him throat long time.

*Raphael, stands, knife poised, looking from Vaughan to Bethan.*

**Rufus:**    Woman, come out of there.

*Rufus grabs Bethan, pushing her forward.*

**Rufus:**    Is this the problem? You can't do it 'cause of she? This woman mek you weak.

*Bethan tries to break free but to no avail.*

**Raphael:**    Let her go!

**Rufus:**    No, Rapha. From time you losing your senses over some white woman. Is her fault this.

*Rufus, holds his knife against Bethan's face.*

**Rufus:**    Perhaps we need to sort her out.

*Vaughan grows anxious, with pent up anger.*

**Vaughan:**    If you touch her! Make him stop.

**Rufus:**    Hush your mouth, you're as good as dead.

*Rose stands between the men.*

**Rose:**    Stop it!

**Rufus:**    Better to take out she and let him come to him senses. Mohammad dead! If he was out there things might be different.

**Rose:**    Let her go!

**Raphael:**    Eh, eh! Is what you try fi say?

**Rufus:**    Dem need you and you in here farcing with some white man. Him almost kill you this morning and you can't put a scratch 'pon him? Let the little rat go if you must, just come out, and lead the men.

**Rose:** Woman, come here. Rufus, let her go.

**Rufus:** No!

**Rose:** Pull yourself together, all of y'all. I won't have an ounce of bloodshed in this house. You know how many men, black and white, must be looking down, wondering what it was all for? Protecting a country and now y'all trying to kill each other in it.

*Rose turns on Vaughan.*

**Rose:** You come in my house, press a knife against my throat, grab me up so. And is you mash up all of this. You don't know me. What kind of a plan is dat you have there? Come round here and just mash up everybody? When the sun come up in the morning, what difference have you really made? Look at the trouble y'causing.

*Rose turns on Raphael.*

**Rose:** And you. Rufus is right. They're your responsibility now. You gone soft? Harden up yourself, and think where you g'wind up if you make one mark 'pon him. What'll happen to everybody, eh?

**Raphael:** I can't let this man just walk out of here.

**Rose:** Is exactly what you're going to do. Let dem go, Raphael. Rufus, let that woman go.

*Rose, slowly approaches Rufus, takes his knife and pulls Bethan free from his arm. She approaches Vaughan with the knife.*

**Rose:** Get up.

*She forces Vaughan towards the door. Raphael, stays close with his knife.*

**Rose:** Now get out.

**Rufus:** Dem probably g' kill him before him step ten paces out of here.

**Rose:** Who knows what g'happen to anyone out there. As long as is not you two do it and under my roof.

*Vaughan stands in the doorway.*

**Vaughan:** Bethan?

**Bethan:** No Vaughan.

**Vaughan:** Come out of this house.

**Bethan:** Go! They've spared your life.

**Vaughan:**   They've spared me nothing.

*Raphael, steps closer to Vaughan, but is forced back by Rose.*

**Raphael:**   Is a big mistake letting him walk out of here.

*Rose, throws a cold glare warning Raphael to stay back.*

**Bethan:**   Go!

**Vaughan:**   (Irate) Why Bethan? You'll throw your life away? Disgrace our family name?

**Bethan:**   Disgrace? You as good as beat me yourself!

**Vaughan:**   You shouldn't be here.

**Bethan:**   (Enraged) You shouldn't be here.

**Vaughan:**   I fought a war, and they are reaping the rewards of it; buying houses when I can barely afford my back room. We're claiming back what's rightfully ours.

*Raphael attempts to break past Rose, but she forces him back again.*

**Rose:**   My husband died in that war.

**Vaughan:**   Most of your men didn't make it past the docks. We took the front line and they took our jobs. We've come home to nothing. And now you want our women too?

**Bethan:**    I'm nobody's possession.

**Vaughan:**  Well not her. Not my sister.

*Vaughan, takes a firm grip of Bethan's arm, pulling her forward towards the door.*

**Bethan:**    Let me go!

*Rufus grabs the knife from Rose's hand. He lunges and cuts Vaughan across the arm. He lifts the knife to Vaughan's face.*

*Vaughan holds his wound tight. He extends his arm offering Bethan one more chance to go with him. They hold a long stare before Bethan's eyes fall to the floor.*

**Vaughan:**  If they find you here, they won't spare you.

*Vaughan points in Bethan's face*

**Vaughan:**  You're nothing but an alien to me now.

*He shifts his pointed finger to Rufus, locks eyes with him and snarls. A smirk appears across Rufus's face, welcoming Vaughan's threatening glare.*

*EXIT* **Vaughan**

*Rufus, looks to Raphael, waiting for his next move. Raphael, points towards the door with his knife and charges forward. Rufus, smirks and falls in line behind him.*

*EXIT* **Rufus** *and* **Raphael**

*Bethan, panicked, runs to the window to see if they are chasing Vaughan.*

**Rose:**    Come from there.

**Bethan:**    But what if they kill him?

*Bethan collapses into the chair, weeping.*

**Rose:**    Kill who? Your brother, or your baby's father? (Pause) Does he know?

*Bethan shakes her head. Rose, approaches the window for a moment before reaching for her shawl.*

**Rose:**    This country has turned on itself, child. Hating, rioting, killing; and it's the same colour blood running through the gutters of the very streets dem fight for.

*Rose moves to Gladys in the drawer, checking her temperature, and wiping her head with a damp cloth.*

**Rose:**    An eye for an eye! That's why we all dying in this pandemic.

*Rose looks to Bethan.*

**Rose:**     The good Lord is weeping with you; I'll tell you dat. I'm going to get my Neci.

*Bethan attempts to stop crying, concerned.*

**Bethan:**   What, you can't leave!

*Rose fires a glance at Bethan.*

**Bethan:**   Is it far?

**Rose:**     You asking me how far I'm willing to go for my own child? You'll soon learn.

*Rose pushes the chair closer to the door leaving a small gap for her to pass through.*

**Rose:**     Close this up behind me. Keep away from the window.

*Bethan prepares to push the chair, panic on her face. Rose looks over at Gladys, then to Bethan, who offers a reassuring look. Rose covers her head with the shawl and looks toward the opening in the door.*

*EXIT* **Rose**

*Bethan pushes the chair against the door. She scans the destruction in the room, picking up a few items and placing them on the side. She picks up the broken photo frame followed by the old photo of Gregory that she used to fan Gladys. She stares at the photo frame and runs a hand across her stomach, clutching her nightgown in anguish. She attempts to place the photo back in the broken frame and places it on the chest of the drawers before reaching to take Gladys out of the drawer.*

*Bethan holds Gladys close to her chest and sits back in the chair.  She rocks gently in the eerie silence, staring at the window. The sound of the riot overwhelms the room.*

FADE TO BLACKOUT

END OF PLAY

# ACKNOWLEDGEMENTS

My heart is overwhelmed with gratitude for my parents.
My Mum, Dr Jill John the powerhouse who nurtures
me, guides me through every milestone
And champions me on.
My Dad, Professor Gus John, for sharpening my
backbone, polishing my armour and sending me out
to fight the good fight;
An activist in my own right.

I am extremely grateful to the John crew,
My siblings who see me through.
My constant supply of love and laughter.
I don't know where or who I'd be without you.
Hope, my jewel, special thanks to you,
For being proof that with the right guidance,
children can live in truth.
Your journey to date is why I create and share
For all to learn; 'We were there!'

Words cannot express my gratitude to my guardian
angel and dear friend Ian,
Whose kindness and generosity know no bounds.
By my side through every season.

Huge thanks to my dearest friend and confidante,
Hannah Wyn Jones, who always makes sure I stay true
to myself, by braving truth with me.
My GPS on my journey.

Immense thanks to my rare and precious publisher,
Your service is Stellar!
No weight in gold could measure.
You're an absolute treasure.

Huge thanks to my love, Dee, who encourages me to fly.
For keeping God at the centre of us all to ensure we
never fall.

Additional thanks and appreciation to:
National Lottery Heritage Fund, Arts Council Wales
and the Wales Millennium Centre.
Gerallt Hughes for his vivid designs, patience and
time.
Chantelle Haugton and DARPL for setting the wheels
in motion and inspiring me to publish and share my
work with the world.

Glory be to God and sincere gratitude to you all.

# ABOUT THE AUTHOR

Author, Ndidi John, is a multidisciplinary artist who has enjoyed a successful career in the creative industries. She has used this platform to support underrepresented communities offering a platform for voice and an opportunity to effect change.

Tiger Bay, Cardiff, is celebrated as one of the oldest multicultural communities in the UK. An industrial dockland and horizon for the world, it is paved with diversity.

Ndidi chose to combine her skills as a playwright and educator to expose one of the most widespread, yet somewhat hidden outbreaks of violence in British history. Her aim is to educate a new generation of audience to the struggles and blood shed for peace on home soil.

Ndidi is committed in her mission to ensure women's voices are heard and respected, for their enduring legacy.  Hence, in an era where male sacrifice is understood and rightfully appreciated, Ndidi focuses on the women, the warriors on the home front.

Ndidi's narrative speaks to a universal audience. Her sincerity and service are crafted to dissolve segregation and promote equality.

My Mother would insist, if it doesn't exist,
Create it, and thrive. That's how I arrived,
At my station.
Through self-direction and project creation.
Fear no-one, do the right thing,
Is the advice my Father would bring.
So simple, yet so profound!
Their wisdom turned my life around.
I stare the impossible in the face,
convince it it has no place.
Around me,
The Queen of possibility.